FILLED WITH THE
SPIRIT
...THEN WHAT?

BY R. MABEL FRANCIS

Filled with the Spirit . . . Then What?
The Christian and Missionary Alliance
One Alliance Place, Reynoldsburg, OH 43068
Copyright © 2025, The Christian and Missionary Alliance

Author: R. Mabel Francis
Foreword by: Steve Grusendorf
Cover Design: David Hardie
Author Photo Illustrations: David Hardie
Interior Design: Matt DeCoste

Scripture taken from the HOLY BIBLE: NEW INTERNATIONAL VERSION. Copyright © 1973, 1978, 1984 by the International Bible Society. Used by permission of Zondervan Bible Publishers.

ISBN: 979-8-9905083-1-6

Printed in the United States of America

FOREWORD

Mabel Francis (1880–1975) was born in Massachusetts in 1880. From the start, she was surrounded by others who served in ministry, including her father and all her uncles. As a teen, she surrendered her life to Jesus while at a Christian camp. She told Him she would go wherever He would send her. The answer would forever change her life. Jesus asked her to go to Japan.

In the early 1900s, when Mabel was in her late twenties, she wrote to A. B. Simpson, the founder of the C&MA, and asked to be sent as a missionary to Japan. At the time, single women weren't permitted to travel for mission work internationally, so Mabel took extra steps to explain her situation—her desire and call—and she paved the way for ministry. Because she was such a successful and mature preacher, Mabel's dream was encouraged in 1909, and she was given permission to go and serve in Japan as a missionary.

Four years later, in 1913, Mabel's brother Tom joined her in Japan, and their sister Anne joined them in 1924. Because of their sacrifice and encouragement, more than 20 churches were established—the gospel was shared in these places that resulted from the work of the sibling trio.

Even when Tom went back to the U.S. and The Alliance withdrew its workers from Japan in 1939, Mabel and Anne decided to remain and continue serving where they felt the Lord calling them. They remained even when hardship almost jeopardized everything.

In 1941, World War II threatened more than just the Francis sisters' ministry; it threatened their very lives—staying in Japan could have meant imprisonment or death. The U.S. and Japanese governments offered the sisters safe passage back to the U.S., but they wanted to remain and help the Japanese once the war was over.

They were certain that the suffering of war would inevitably bring an openness to the gospel—a hope and assurance that kept them in Japan. They weren't mistaken; many opportunities arose. The same year that the war began, Mabel turned her house into a clinic in order to tend to the sick. She joined Anne a year later in an internment camp near Tokyo, and they stayed there for three long years.

As the war heightened, so did the effects of such brutality. Bombs fell, fires engulfed their camp, and they narrowly escaped the dangerous and treacherous conditions that intensely threatened their lives. While she witnessed the horrible suffering by the morning light, Mabel wrote that her hope was continuously in the Lord. She was not relying on her own strength but the strength that only He could give to her.

That very strength brought Mabel to continue to minister to the Japanese people in their suffering, through their deepest pain and trials. She traveled all over Japan giving witness of the Lord's goodness and provision, desiring to present the hope of the good news and to rebuild the church. As the devastating atomic bombing of Hiroshima

wrecked the city and its people, Mabel was there leading
many survivors to Christ, and she organized a church and
a Bible school. Out of the wreckage, she rebuilt pieces for
the Lord's glory.

Over the four years that followed the war, Mabel and
Anne planted six churches, a Bible school, multiple grade
schools, orphanages, and medical clinics. They knew that
they couldn't do it on their own, so Mabel wrote to the
C&MA missions board and requested that they send
workers back to Japan. Mabel was there to welcome them
when they arrived, and once more, writing to the C&MA
brought Kingdom impact to a somewhat unreached and
broken people group.

Mabel's efforts were, of course, for the glory of God, but
all that she did and accomplished did not go unnoticed by
others, even the local Japanese government. The Japanese
emperor held a ceremony for Mabel on May 7, 1962, in
which he presented her with the 5th Order of the Sacred
Treasure, the highest honor Japan gives to a foreigner,
awarded to those who have made incredible impact and
achievement. She was recognized for how she helped the
Japanese people in their lowest, most distressing moments
and for how she led hundreds to know more about Christ.

Mabel's declaration of faith in the Lord was evident in
the ways she followed God's calling on her life, led others
to know Him, and aided the broken in their greatest time
of need.

After her retirement from the mission field, Mabel,
who had learned the practical path of the "crucified life"
while serving as a missionary for many years, penned this
short work.

What is the crucified life, you ask? It is a life of spiritual victory that becomes a reality to the Christian who is willing to put to death their own self-life and identify with the death and Resurrection of Jesus Christ.

This simple yet powerful work is a thoughtful, down-to-earth, honest look at what it takes to walk in the fullness of the Holy Spirit. It is simply the heart and mind of a missionary and daughter of Christ on display. If you are curious to really know what the deeper life looks like and how it is gained, this book will satisfy your search.

Dr. Steve Grusendorf
Director, Alliance Center for Leadership Development

Studies in Alliance Thought is a curated collection of works designed to help the modern Christian and Missionary Alliance family stay deeply connected to our historical and theological roots as a holiness and missionary movement. Drawing from the rich writings of past and present Alliance pastors, theologians, and missionaries, this collection serves as both a reminder of where we've been and a guide for where the Lord is leading us as an Alliance movement. By revisiting the timeless truths of our past and reflecting on our present, this series aims to equip and inspire a new generation to live out the deeper life and fulfill the Great Commission.

TABLE OF CONTENTS

CHAPTER I:

AM I REALLY ANXIOUS FOR A LIFE OF VICTORY?

"I must take the path "down" that Jesus took!

On the plane coming home to "retire," after a long and happy ministry to the dear Japanese people, the Lord said to me:

"I have a new commission for you. You have followed me in Japan. Now I want you to tell the people at home what I have taught you."

That was a number of years ago, and although I had thought that I could never leave Japan, I must confess that I have been even happier in my home ministry telling people everywhere of the gracious secrets of spiritual victory over the ugly "self" life within us.

Many of God's dear people have by faith received the fullness of the Holy Spirit but they still find themselves being impatient, especially in the home.

Many become irritated when they are falsely accused or slandered. They give way to sensitiveness and self-pity.

They begin to wonder: "Why should I have all these difficulties? Didn't I receive the fullness of the Holy Spirit as an act of faith after all?"

Doubt and confusion and discouragement seem to follow these questions. So they go back over their experience with critical evaluation, and many seem to be living under a sense of condemnation as a result.

My own personal testimony about earlier years of my Christian life, and even the earlier years of my missionary service, includes the same kind of struggles and conflicts that perplex many in our churches today.

I knew that I had definitely received the fullness of the Holy Spirit into my life and into my being. So, during many times of testing, I, too, wondered why the same old conflicts and discouragements would arise within me.

Beloved, it is right here that many of us make our mistake. The truth is that the Holy Spirit does not make us humanly perfect and does not guarantee that we will automatically spend the rest of our lives on a spiritual mountaintop!

I think that many Christians honestly do not realize that the Spirit of God wants to show them their own self-life as God sees it. There cannot be full spiritual victory within any individual who is not willing to deal with that ugly life of self, applying God's own prescription of complete identification with the death of Jesus Christ.

The path of death is humbling, but what about the road that Jesus followed?

He went straight to the cross. Straight to death!

Jesus humbled Himself and became a man—and I tell you, that was really humbling for the Son of God.

He was the Creator—but He was willing to come to us in the form of the created being. We can never fully know what that meant.

Then He became as a servant, the lowest of men, without even a place to lay His head.

In this humility, He became obedient even unto death, the death of the cross.

And isn't that what our Lord asks of us?

"And whosoever doth not bear his cross, and come after me, cannot be my disciple," said Jesus.

Don't you see that the blessed outcome of His humility, His willingness to take the path "down," His death on the cross, was this: "Wherefore God hath highly exalted Him"—our Lord Jesus Christ is on the highest seat that anyone could ever take.

He is in the glory! He lives! He is there ruling and reigning!

The only way that we can know His victory and His glory is just to let Him come in His fullness and take over. If we do not acknowledge this secret as the means of dealing with sin and self, we will never experience the gracious fulfillment of our being made one with Him, fused in our nature in oneness with the divine nature of our victor, Jesus Christ.

We receive the fullness of the Holy Spirit by faith. He comes into our hearts and we know that He has come. He comes to teach us of Christ and He wants to show us what we are in terms of our old self-life. He wants to show us so Christ can take over the reins, and He will keep knocking at any little door in your life that you have closed off for yourself!

Questions for Self-Reflection

1. In what areas of your life do you find yourself still struggling with impatience, self-pity, or defensiveness, even after receiving the fullness of the Holy Spirit? How can you invite God to transform these parts of your "self" life?

2. The path of humility and self-denial is central to following Christ. How does Jesus' journey to the cross challenge the way you view your own struggles and sacrifices in daily life? What specific actions might God be asking you to take in order to fully surrender your "self" to Him?

3. When you face discouragement or doubt about your spiritual growth, how do you typically respond? How can recognizing the continued work of the Holy Spirit in revealing areas of your life for surrender bring you peace and victory instead of frustration?

CHAPTER 2

DO I HOLD THE IDEA THAT I AM COMPLETE IN MYSELF?

Jesus wants to become my "completeness"!

Many people receive the fullness of the Holy Spirit with marvelous blessing and victory—and then, because of failure to keep their eyes on Jesus as their overcoming portion, they have found everything around them gray and dim once more!

What was that water—that "supply"—that Jesus promised to the woman at the well in the Gospel of John?

Jesus was really saying to her: "I will give you Myself!"

He did not promise that she would have an experience that would keep her from "thirsting" again. Any Christian who believes that there is some kind of an emotional "binge" that results in continuing spiritual victory will soon be floundering again.

The Scriptures tell us plainly that we must get our eyes away from human experience and feeling. Then, looking only to our Lord Jesus Christ, His Spirit and His victory become a spring bubbling up into everlasting life!

Where is the problem, then?

Instead of looking at the mighty resurrection power of the Lord Jesus, people go back to looking at themselves—and that's why they lose hope and give in so easily to defeat and discouragement.

Beloved, we are actually dealing here with Christ's supernatural power—not with just our human hopes and resolutions!

How can I be so sure of this kind of divine supply?

In Ephesians 3:16, I read this proof: "May He grant you out of the rich treasury of His glory to be strengthened and reinforced with mighty power in the inner man by the (Holy) Spirit [Himself]—indwelling your innermost being and personality" (Amplified New Testament).

"He will strengthen and reinforce."

We are right up against the awful conflict of the ages and no ordinary power will avail. However, we may be reinforced within by the Holy Spirit's indwelling our inner being and personality. This is possible because Christ, the living Christ, dwells within us and makes His permanent home in our hearts.

This is the reason for my great joy. Oh, what a glorious privilege to be able to tell God's people of the wonderful years of blessing I have known since I found the secret of letting God take over. This is a moment-by-moment experience of reckoning and faith.

Even when we are weak and fail so often, He has promised that when He is allowed to come in and take over, it is the fulfillment of our being made one with Him!

I have often thought that it is very much like the "gold-filled" process that we hear about in the jewelry trade.

I have a gold-filled watch—but it is not solid gold! The men in that craft heat up their little furnaces. They melt a certain amount of gold and they also melt a supply of iron—and then they fuse the two elements together.

My watch is not just gold-plated, it is gold-filled. The gold is fused with the iron and it will never wear off. You see, it is just as nice as if it were all gold. The two metals are fused together and they become one in substance.

Can you see, as I do, that this is a picture of our going on with God in the trials and conflicts and discouragements of life until we get melted down and reckon ourselves to have died with Christ—and so we get fused in with the person and the nature of our Lord Jesus Christ.

This becomes the secret of His victorious indwelling—you don't know which is which. By faith and by desire and by commitment, we are just one with Him.

But this is what we have to remember—we must be willing to be melted down before we can be fused with Him in His humility and in His death and resurrection.

This is the spiritual lesson about which we cannot argue. If we want to have this glorious life of victory, the pathway is down, farther down, all the way down.

But, as we must go down with Him into His death, so it will be with our identification with Him in His resurrection and glory.

Colossians 1:27 is actually God's plan for our lives: "To whom God would make known what is the riches of the glory of this mystery among the Gentiles; which is CHRIST IN YOU, THE HOPE OF GLORY."

This is our inheritance from God, and I am so anxious for everyone to know this life of victory because it is for us, beloved!

Perhaps it may be with you like it was with me: I found that Jesus Himself wanted to be my "completeness"—and I had been wanting to be complete in myself!

Self-Reflection Questions:

1. In what areas of your life are you still seeking to be complete in yourself, rather than allowing Jesus to be your "completeness"? How might you surrender those areas to Him and trust in His sufficiency?

2. How do you respond when you experience discouragement or spiritual dryness after moments of victory? What steps can you take to keep your eyes on Christ's resurrection power rather than your own limitations?

3. What does it mean for you personally to be "melted down" and fused with Christ in His death and resurrection? How can you embrace humility and surrender as part of your daily walk with Him?

CHAPTER 3

IS IT GOOD ADVICE THAT I SHOULD "CRUCIFY" MYSELF?

The blessed secret: "I am crucified with Christ"!

For many years I quoted the Bible verse, "I am crucified with Christ," and preached from it, too, when it was merely a picture in my mind and I had not come to know the reality of identification with Him in His death.

I have heard people say in spiritual counsel: "You must crucify yourself!"

But you do not have the power to crucify yourself. More than likely you will pet yourself!

Beloved, most of us are not willing to admit how very dear "self" is to us. This is where the battle is taking place and this is where we need to acknowledge the work of the Holy Spirit within us.

I am happy to have had the privilege of telling many people in the homeland what God had revealed to me. He showed me that the Holy Spirit had come not only to give me power but also to shed light all through my being so I could recognize the traits of the old self-life.

It was the Holy Spirit who revealed to me that the only way to deal with self in our spiritual life is by death—and death does not come easy!

It was in this light that the Spirit of God revealed to me why the Lord Jesus could not have been slain in a moment. He had to get into the place of death and stay there until death came.

While He was nailed to the cross the crowd shouted to Him to come down. If He would do this, they said, they would believe that He was the Messiah. But He was drinking a bitter cup and He knew that He had to stay there until He was dead—six long hours!

If we could die immediately in regard to self, it would be much easier!

However, we need time to see all the traits of self and to consign them to the cross one by one—until we have died to all of them. That is what makes it hard.

But how blessed to know now, that instead of going into a spiritual slump when I saw these traits of self, I was to thank God for showing them to me and bring them directly to Him and trust Him to give deliverance at every point.

Each time God shows you anything that remains of the old life of self, bring it to Him immediately if you are really concerned about spiritual victory and the overcoming life.

There will always be the inner temptation: "I will deal with it tomorrow!"

Deal with it now. Do not put it aside. Do not excuse it. Let Christ take over in the entire situation, for this assurance of victory and deliverance is possible only when He is allowed to be in control through His Spirit.

This is the kind of Christlike control and direction that people saw in Sophie the scrubwoman who was a power for God in the New York Alliance Tabernacle a generation ago.

"I am determined that I am going to have everything that is in the Father's will for me, regardless of what the rest of the heirs say,'" she would declare. Because she was willing to die out to everything that she might call her own, she bore much fruit for her Savior.

Jesus said that if a corn of wheat falls into the ground and dies, it brings forth much fruit. We are more likely to think that we can work for Jesus and bring forth fruit by "doing."

But Jesus said: "If it die!"

I read years ago that an Egyptian mummy entombed for three thousand years or more was found to have a few grains of wheat in his hand when the wrappings were taken off. Scientists wondered if this wheat would sprout and grow, so the kernels were taken to Canada's great wheat-growing country. They were planted in the proper season and several of the kernels did sprout and grow and reproduce. During the next season these were used as seed again and they reproduced more wheat.

For three thousand years those grains of wheat were completely dormant; because they were not put into the ground to die, they fed no one. But when they were planted and died, they brought forth fruit and now they are feeding multitudes.

Oh, how much easier it would have been if I had known the secret of death to my old self-life and the blessed secret of spiritual fruit-bearing when I first went to Japan.

I was anxious about many things and, ultimately, the Lord revealed to me that anxiety was sin and hindered His working.

He said to me: "You ask for something and then you proceed to tie My hands by your anxiety." It is His work—and it is my business to believe Him. No strain or stress is necessary. He is over all. It is no longer I, but Christ who dwells within!

Gerhard Tersteegen's hymn expresses this glorious truth:

Is there a thing beneath the sun
That strives with thee my heart to share?
Ah, tear it thence, and reign alone,
The Lord of every motion there;
Then shall my heart from earth be free,
When it hath found repose in Thee.

Self-Reflection Questions:

1. In what areas of your life do you still try to rely on your own efforts or strength to achieve spiritual growth, rather than surrendering to the work of Christ and the Holy Spirit? How can you trust God more fully in those areas?

2. What specific traits of your "self-life" is the Holy Spirit revealing to you? How can you bring these areas to Christ and allow Him to bring about transformation and victory?

3. Are there any anxieties or burdens you are holding onto that may be hindering God's work in your life? How can you release those to Him, trusting that "it is no longer I, but Christ who dwells within"?

CHAPTER 4

DOES GOD DEAL WITH ASPECTS OF THE SELF-LIFE IN CHILDREN?

Envy and irritation and pride have no age limits!

In looking back upon my childhood in New England and my experiences as a Christian girl and young woman, it is very plain to me that I had some personal traits and characteristics with which God had to deal specifically before my life was adequate for service in His great work.

I am going to refer to such attitudes as envy, irritability, disobedience, self-pity, impatience, pride, selfishness, sensitivity, and slowness to forgive.

My life has been peculiarly guided and directed by God. He placed me in a genuine Christian home where my devout parents looked always to God in the rearing of their four daughters and three sons. Regular family prayers and grace at meals gave each of us the foundation for our lives. How thankful I am to God for placing me in such a Christian environment and for making provisions for training me for the work He wanted me to do.

When I was seven years old, Father called my sister Gertrude and me to him. He said, "Now, girls, you are old enough to help your mother. Gertrude, I want you to wash the dishes after each meal. Mabel, you are to dry them."

I hated to dry dishes and I found many ways to avoid it. One day after dinner, I complained about a stomachache. Mother said she would dry the dishes in my place. As I saw my tired mother doing my work I felt greatly condemned. I asked God to help me. He certainly did because after this I did not rebel when it came time to do the work.

Shortly after this Father was holding a tent meeting and he invited those who were really sorry for their sins to come to the front. I went down the outside aisle to the altar. No one paid any attention to me. I knelt there and asked God's forgiveness for my sins. I also asked God to help me to overcome my hatred of doing housework. After that I tried to live as I felt a Christian should.

Later, Father remarked about my changed disposition, saying, "How happy I am to see such a good helper around the house!"

I had to learn many lessons about how the Lord molds a Christian into a person He can use. I dedicated my life to God, but still I felt something was missing in my life. This troubled me because I could not figure out what my problem could be.

I was really too young at that time to know the full meaning of the word *envy,* but I know that I was troubled about my facial features.

People often remarked about my sister: "Isn't Gertrude beautiful!"

But no one ever said, "Isn't Mabel beautiful!" and this was of great concern to me.

But the Lord did show me that this was really envy, and He dealt with it in my life by giving me an understanding of the great work Queen Esther had done for her people. It was not Esther's beautiful face that counted and made the difference. It was the fact that she was faithful and willing to die that saved her people from death and ruin. It seemed to me that I could envision what would have happened if Esther had failed. She certainly would have heard the cry of her people as they were being slaughtered.

At that point God spoke to me: "If you are not faithful to your call, you will hear the wail of souls going into a Christless eternity." Further, He said: "There is a work for you to do that no one else in all the world can do. There will be a lack in My great plan if you are unfaithful."

During a long illness of my father it was necessary for him to leave home for treatment, and Mother accompanied him. I was placed in charge of my younger brothers and sisters. When they didn't obey my commands I became vexed and irritable. One night after the children had gone to bed, I went to see if they were all right. I noticed that one brother had been crying; a big tear was standing on his cheek.

I knew that I had caused his crying. I was so convicted that I knelt by his bed and asked God to forgive me. I began to think how kind and thoughtful of others Mother was. I prayed, "Oh God, help me to be more considerate of the feelings of others."

This proved a valuable lesson—a lesson to be learned over and over, not only before I went to Japan but also after I started my work there.

Self-Reflection Questions:

1. Looking back on your own childhood or early life, can you identify traits like envy, pride, or irritability that God has worked on within you? How has He helped you grow in those areas?

2. In what ways might God be working on your "self-life" now, especially in areas where you still struggle with emotions like impatience, selfishness, or sensitivity? How can you invite Him to continue molding you?

3. Like Mabel, do you sometimes struggle with comparing yourself to others or feeling inadequate? How can you shift your focus to being faithful to God's unique calling for your life, rather than focusing on outward appearances or abilities?

CHAPTER 5

How can I show God that I really want to please Him?

I can love Him completely instead of loving myself!

It was not until after I had left home at the age of fifteen to further my education that I learned what the Bible says about the person and the work of the Holy Spirit.

As I read the Word of God, I found that the Holy Spirit is given to those who obey God (Acts 5:32). Now, to me, this meant to obey Him for life. A fierce conflict raged within my heart. How could I say, "Yes, Lord, I will obey," when I did not know what He would ask me to do? I did not understand at that time that He would faithfully lead me *step by step!*

But first God dealt with me about a very personal matter. He asked me if I were willing to be different from other girls, to give up trying to be outwardly attractive and to just live for Him. I knew then that I should be more simple in my manner of dress and to think less about my personal appearance. I did not have any fine clothes but

I saw the desire of my heart was to look pretty and to be admired by my friends.

At that time I wore bangs and spent much time curling them with a hot iron. Whenever it rained the curl would just disappear. This disturbed me and I kept thinking constantly about my appearance. I was distressed when God told me to comb my hair straight back. When I looked in the mirror I thought, "How terrible I look!"

I asked the Lord if He really wanted me to look like this. He replied that it looked beautiful to Him. I still hoped that He would change His mind—but He didn't.

God kept asking me, "Do you really want to please Me?" I would answer, "Yes, but…" One day I reasoned that if I looked so terrible I would not have a friend on earth. This was such a tremendous battle to me that I became ill and could not meet anyone.

How I praise God for revealing Himself to me through the words of Jesus, "When I was in the Garden of Gethsemane sweating drops of blood for you I was alone (Luke 22:41-44). Aren't you willing to go alone with Me?"

This broke my heart, and I said, "Yes, Lord, I am and I will."

The blessed Holy Spirit came into my heart in His fullness. Everything seemed changed. There came to me such a burden for people without a knowledge of Christ, people who were *lost,* that I could not rest. Everything was different. The awfulness of a soul being lost was made very real to me.

During my early teaching days I suffered the loss of a very dear friend. How much of my time I spent mourning his loss!

God spoke to me very clearly as I sat by his grave: "You are the only one in this area who knows My love and who has tasted salvation and here you are grieving for this one who you know has gone to heaven." He asked me to put aside this grief and to open a meeting at the school on Sunday afternoons. I was to invite the people to come and then to tell those who came of His salvation. I was startled, but the call was clear and I obeyed. I sent out invitations by the children asking the parents to come.

Before the end of the school year many of those dear country people had found Christ as their personal Savior. The news of these meetings spread to nearby villages. Thus, my Christian ministry was started.

I was nineteen years old and holding evangelistic meetings in Haverhill, Massachusetts, when the Lord spoke clearly to me and gave me a vision of the great nation of Japan. Now I knew where God wanted me to serve—and I was glad!

Self-Relfection Questions:

1. What personal desires, habits, or attachments are you holding onto that may hinder your ability to fully please God? How can you surrender those areas and trust that God will lead you step by step, even when the path seems uncertain?

2. Are there moments in your life where you feel called to stand out or be different for the sake of obedience to God? How do you respond to those moments, and what steps can you take to show your willingness to live for Him rather than for the approval of others?

3. How has God revealed Himself to you during times of personal struggle or sacrifice? How can you be more open to following His call, even when it requires leaving behind your own plans or desires?

CHAPTER 6

WHAT CAN I DO ABOUT A CHRONIC LACK OF PATIENCE?

I have to confess my failure and seek the Lord!

Now that my decision had been made to go to Japan, how anxious I was to get there and start the work of telling the Japanese about my wonderful Savior!

But my patience was tested. First, there was the matter of accumulating funds sufficient for my rail ticket to Seattle, the sea passage to Japan, and support for the first year. Also, there were problems of anticipating and collecting my personal effects for life in Japan.

Second, the trip by sea took almost a month and during much of it I was seasick. I felt that I was wasting precious time!

Third, I was an American; therefore, I had to be quarantined on my arrival in Japan. This problem was soon solved, however, for on the second day the American consul, whom I had met on the crossing, requested the authorities to allow me to come to his hotel and take care of his wife, who was ill. While there I was able to find time for prayer and to fully recover from the effects of the long voyage.

Fourth, how troublesome I found the communication problem! I knew not one word of Japanese and it seemed to take so long to learn just a little. How much time I felt was being lost before I could start my work!

There were no language schools at that time. The only way to learn the language was to sit down and study. A young girl who had just been graduated from grammar school came at nine o'clock every morning and would instruct me in the language until five o'clock in the afternoon. When I learned a few words I would try to put them into a sentence. She would guess what I was trying to say and correct me. If she guessed wrong, I learned wrong. However, she was a bright girl and that helped greatly.

Another thing bothered me and made me impatient: in the early days travel in Japan was very slow. The trains went at the enormous rate of fifteen miles an hour, and everything else seemed just as slow. There were no buses and no cars. (Of course, we didn't have many cars in America then either.) It was often necessary to travel by rickshaw that went only as fast as a man could run. That was not fast enough to suit me! I bought a bicycle so that I could pedal fast and go over the mountains. But, oh, I became so frustrated and so impatient!

Then there were many things about the culture and traditions of the Japanese that I did not understand. I couldn't understand why certain things had to be done in a certain way.

Some of the things the girls did seemed impractical and sometimes even wrong. One girl who helped me was very trying. When washing the stairs she would start from the bottom and walk up on the wet stairs as she washed them. I explained to her that it would be better if she would start at the top and wash down because she would not leave her foot marks on the stairs.

But she would say, "Well, I like my way better," and would continue to do the work her way. It seemed to me that if there were any possible wrong way for her to do a task, she would do it that way.

One morning as I was going to prayer meeting the words of James 1:2 came to me: "Count it all joy when you fall into divers temptations." The Lord asked me, "Are you counting it all joy about this girl?"

I replied, "No, Lord, I'm counting it very trying."

This girl was an orphan and I knew she had nowhere to go if I should dismiss her. However, when I had won the victory over all the little annoyances that came because she always wanted her own way of doing things, she left and God sent me another girl. I began to realize that God was, and is, in all things!

The Japanese attitude toward the time element was also very different from mine. I became annoyed when the girls and my helpers did not appear "on time." One day I told my girl to have dinner ready at exactly twelve o'clock because I expected a guest. When I came home from a meeting and discovered that the dinner was not ready, I was very perturbed and told her plainly that she had disobeyed me.

But God said to me: "If you had been in the kitchen yourself this morning, you couldn't have done any better. She had one hindrance after another. When things don't go your way you blame others."

It was so easy for me to blame others when the circumstances were unknown or misunderstood. The Lord was waiting for me to bring this problem to Him. He assures us His deliverance is always available but only after we have reached the end of our own self- assertion.

Self-Reflection Questions:

1. How do you typically respond when things don't go according to your plan or when progress seems slow? What steps can you take to surrender your impatience to God and trust His timing in these moments?

2. In what situations do you find yourself blaming others for frustrations or delays? How might you approach those situations differently, seeking God's perspective and grace instead of reacting out of impatience?

3. Are there specific areas of your life where God might be using difficult circumstances or people to teach you patience and humility? How can you be more open to learning from these challenges rather than becoming frustrated by them?

CHAPTER 7

WHAT MAKES ME NASTY AND UNPLEASANT TO OTHERS?

I have not let the Spirit of God show me my own heart!

After I began to speak the Japanese language a little better, the mission assigned a Bible woman to help me in the role of co-worker.

One day I said to her, "Now this morning we'll go out to certain places to call."

She replied, "Yes, but just let me go and give the pastor an answer to a question he asked me. It won't take me but five minutes."

I waited two hours. During that time I imagined many things that they must have been discussing. Among other topics I was sure that they were talking about me. I became very much upset. When my co-worker did return she said, "Oh Sensei, I'm so sorry I kept you waiting all this time."

If only I had said, "Never mind, we'll go now," all would have gone smoothly. I could not say that because I was wrought up inside. I do not remember what I said, but I do know that it was something nasty.

God continued to deal with me about this failure. I saw that it was self—something I had not realized before. I saw that my commitment to God had not been complete. I found myself becoming very impatient because there seemed to be so many difficulties to overcome.

A few days later I was reading Andrew Murray's book on humility. He wrote:

Humility is perfect quietness of heart. It is to have no trouble. It is never to be fretted, vexed, irritated, sore or disappointed. It is to expect nothing, to wonder at nothing that is done to me, to feel nothing done against me. It is to be at rest when nobody praises me, and when I am blamed and despised. It is to have a blessed home in the Lord where I can go in and shut the door and kneel to my Father in secret. I am at peace as in a deep sea of calmness when all around is trouble.

Every word of this definition pierced my heart. I had thought I was humble, but I knew then that I did not know the first thing about humility. I would get fretful, vexed, sore, and disappointed. I seemed to be all undone!

Time and again I had to fight against this great impatience of mine. Here is another example. After I had moved to a large, rambling house 1 kept a box of pencils on a table in the entrance where I often stopped to write down an address or some note that I wanted to remember. One day I put another box there and said to the girls who worked for me: "Now if you break the lead of one of these pencils, please put it in this second box." I explained that when I was in a rush to write something it would avoid picking up a pencil with no lead. They said, "Oh, yes, we understand."

One morning not long after a gentleman came to the door. "I have only a minute," he said, "please take down this address." I rushed to the box of pencils. 1 picked up one pencil after another that had no lead. As I picked up the seventh pencil, the last one in the box, and saw the broken lead, 1 gave it an impatient toss. Then I found a pencil and wrote the address the man gave me; but immediately the Holy Spirit said, "I was grieved when you threw the pencil down in that manner."

After the man left, I called my helpers and said, "Girls, I want you to pray for me. I have grieved the Holy Spirit and it is no light thing." I told them what I had done; I wept and prayed. They wept and prayed. I did not say, "You put the pencils in the wrong box." That really had nothing to do with it. I had been impatient. I had acted in this way because of an impatient trait down inside that had to be dealt with.

I told the Lord about this, and I never have felt this impatient attitude from that day to this.

The Lord said, "When you see any working of this old self-nature bring it to Me and I'll put it on the cross and it will be gone." It is very important when we are dealing with the traits of the *self-life* that we do not make excuses for them or try to vindicate ourselves.

No matter what comes up, God takes it to the cross when we let Him deal definitely with our old self-nature. God also said to me at that time, "I never let anything come into the life of My child unless I have a reason. I have undertaken to perfect you. I have undertaken to bring you into the place of complete deliverance. Everything I let come into your life is purposeful."

I learned to ask not why some things happened but, "What is God doing now? What is He trying to teach me through this particular situation?"

Another area in which God dealt with me was concerning selfishness and sensitivity. Some of us seem to have our nerves on the outside and we get hurt very easily. It is not the things that hurt, it is YOU that God wants to deal with! He wants to show you where self is residing. God let me go through more difficult experiences before I learned the spiritual lessons He wanted me to learn!

Self-Reflection Questions:

1. When you experience impatience or irritation, how often do you look inward to examine your heart and see if it's revealing a deeper issue of self? How can you allow the Holy Spirit to bring these tendencies to the cross for transformation?

2. In what situations do you tend to react defensively or harshly, and how might God be using these moments to teach you humility and patience? How can you respond differently by seeking His peace instead of reacting out of frustration?

3. Are there areas in your life where you are quick to blame others for mistakes or annoyances, rather than recognizing how your own impatience or selfishness might be at play? What steps can you take to let God deal with those traits instead of justifying or excusing them?

CHAPTER 8

WHAT IF I HAVE A HYPERSENSITIVE, SUSPICIOUS NATURE?

I will always be unhappy until I yield it to God!

I wonder if God ever had to deal with you because you were oversensitive in areas where you felt you were not properly "appreciated."

This was one of my problem attitudes in Japan.

After my brother Tom came to Japan as a missionary, we decided that it was time to organize the Alliance church in Japan. We were happy to have a group of fine, educated men who seemed to be dedicated to the Lord. The church was organized and everything went smoothly and according to plan.

But I began to feel very lonely and a little on the outside because I had less responsibility than before. One Sunday morning when I went into the church, the pastor and one of the deacons who were engaged in conversation stopped talking as I entered. In my sensitivity and desire to be noticed, I thought they did not want me to hear what they were saying; I felt very much left out.

So I asked the Lord: "What is the cause of this ugly feeling? Please show me!"

It was quite some days before the Lord revealed the reason. It came to me as I was reading Matthew 20:28: "The Son of man came not to be ministered unto, but to minister, and to give his life a ransom for many." I had read that passage many times before. My reaction was: of course, I did not want to be ministered unto!

When people came to tie my shoes (we had to remove our shoes when we entered a house in Japan), I did not want them to do it. When people would give me a cushion, I knew they would sit on the bare floor. I did not need the cushion. I could sit on the bare floor, too. I did not want to be ministered unto!

But the Holy Spirit showed me that although I did not expect people to wait on me physically, I did like them to minister to my old *self-life*. I liked them to say, "We are so glad you're here this morning; we wouldn't know what to do without you. We must have your opinion."

The Lord Jesus reminded me of His own ministry by saying, "I wasn't ministered unto, and after I had healed and blessed people, nobody said, 'Thank you.' Instead they gave Me a crown of thorns and a cross. They took My life. And I want you to follow in My footsteps. They are not going to thank you and you don't need thanks. Whenever there is something to do, do it gladly and then get out of the way."

One day as I was praying God showed me as in a vision a leaf fall to the ground and decay right before my eyes and become fertilizer for the tree. God said, "From now on I want you to become 'fertilizer' for this church." Now nobody goes around praising fertilizer. No one ever says, "What wonderful fertilizer!"

When I was in charge of the church I did the things I wanted to do and gave the unwanted tasks to someone else. A leader can sometimes be very selfish. I was filled with deep conviction regarding my lack of the demonstration of the Holy Spirit. But then, when I cast myself upon God, glad hallelujahs filled my soul as He gave blessed release. "He whom the Son makes free is free indeed."

From that time on it made no difference whether I performed the task or someone else did. I realized that it was God's work and that I really did not have anything to do with it except to obey Him.

God richly blessed the little church and caused it to grow.

Self-Reflection Questions:

1. In what areas of your life do you find yourself seeking affirmation or appreciation from others? How might God be calling you to release this need and focus instead on serving without expectation of recognition or praise?

2. When you feel excluded or overlooked, how do you typically respond? How can you shift your focus from self to Christ's example of humility, as He came to serve without seeking acknowledgment?

3. Are there responsibilities or tasks that you avoid because they don't offer recognition or personal satisfaction? How can you embrace a heart of service, like the "fertilizer" in the passage, willing to support others and God's work even when unnoticed?

CHAPTER 9

WHAT ABOUT FALSE RUMORS AFFECTING MY REPUTATION?

"Not one word in defense" and "Be ready to forgive!"

In many ways the Holy Spirit continued to probe deeper into my inner life.

Being a single lady and a missionary, I was very zealous to maintain a good reputation. One of the ladies in the mission wanted her husband to be president of the work. While my brother, who was president, was on furlough she thought if she could get me off the field, too, everything would be in her favor. In order to accomplish this she told a story that I was not living morally. She even wrote to the New York Board; they sent out a representative to check this report.

When I heard about this (someone is always kind enough to tell you when there is a rumor about you), the Lord instructed me: "You are not to say one word or try to vindicate yourself." Oh, how I longed to say one word at least, but the Lord said, "Not one word! You are not even to let anyone know that you have heard the rumor. Your business in the midst of this is to die to self, even to your reputation."

I continually prayed, "Lord, give me grace." I was not very happy and neither was I rejoicing in the Lord. Matthew 5:11-12 says that when men speak evil against us, we should "rejoice, and be exceeding glad." Although I went through this trial, I almost lost my health. I did not want to go out or to meet people because I wondered if they had heard the rumor.

I asked the Lord about this attitude and how I should react. His answer came to me one Sunday morning during a church service when a young man read Colossians 3:13: "If any man have a quarrel against any: even as Christ forgave you, so also do ye." The Japanese translation of the Scripture is very clear: "If any man have a cause to blame another, forgive him." As the Holy Spirit illumined the Word, I looked up to God and said, "Lord, I will; I do."

This experience not only upset me, but it brought to light envy, jealousy, and suspicion that I didn't know was in my heart. Those traits were there—no question about that. Then the Lord Jesus said, "You didn't know but I knew, and I purposely brought this experience to you that you might see these traits." I was deeply moved when I thought of the pains that God was taking to train and to teach me. I thanked Him for showing me this condition.

The Lord revealed to me that the Adamic nature—the self-life—must be met by death. I had thought that when I was cleansed by the blood of Jesus and filled with the Holy Spirit all the self-life was taken away. He showed me that His method of dealing with the self- life was not just cleansing, it was crucifixion.

Death of the old is necessary for new life and fruit. "Except a corn of wheat fall into the ground and die, it abideth alone: but if it die, it bringeth forth much fruit" (John 12:24). Oh, how these words pierced my soul! I said, "Lord Jesus, I don't know how to die." In desperation I cried, "Teach me to die!"

Again God spoke to me, this time through Matthew 16:24: "If any man will come after me [be my disciple], let him deny himself, and take up his cross, and follow me." I had never understood that passage. Many times I had asked what God meant by denying one's self. I knew He did not mean for me to deny my existence, for even if I said, "I am not here," I still was.

Now the meaning of this Scripture was clear to me: *self* should have no place whatever. Now I understood that self was to die. But I didn't know how to die! In my desperation I cried again, "Teach me to die!"

God's instructions were that every time there was an uprising of *self* I was to go to Him directly, immediately, and without making any excuse whatever. I was to confess it to Him. I saw that I had been excusing myself for these traits and actions.

Sometimes when you get angry with someone, you say, "I know I shouldn't have, but they shouldn't have done what they did either!" You don't get anywhere that way. But if you take the matter to the Lord, He will take it away. When someone hurts you, bring it immediately to God. Do not take time to tell your best friend before bringing it to the Lord.

God said, "I'll bring experiences into your life that are necessary for you to see where *self* is hiding. You are unable to see *self* but I will show you." God knows every place where *self* works in our lives. It seemed to me at this time that every part of my being was stained with this old *self.* God exposed one trait after another, showed it to me, and brought it to the cross.

When you really forgive a wrong, it is gone. True forgiveness does not put it away on the shelf to bring out at some other time. When I said, "I do forgive," I was liberated. Gone was the feeling of sensitivity about meeting people. Gone was the resentment toward those who had hurt me.

Unutterable joy filled my soul with this blessed release! It is wonderful to be forgiven, but it is more wonderful to forgive.

Still, though this was a blessed victory, it was not the end. But knowing that I was in the will of God made me very happy.

Self-Reflection Questions:

1. When false rumors or misunderstandings arise about you, how do you typically respond? Are you quick to defend yourself, or do you bring the situation to God and trust Him to handle it?

2. In moments when you're hurt by others' actions or words, how readily do you forgive? Are there any past hurts or offenses that you're still holding onto that need to be brought to God for true forgiveness and release?

3. How does your desire for approval or a good reputation affect your interactions with others? How can you shift your focus from preserving your reputation to denying self and following Christ's example of humility and forgiveness?

CHAPTER 10

How can I know that self has gone to the cross?

Ask God in humility for His revelation of resurrection life!

Shortly after this experience, feeling the need to be alone and rest, I went up to Karuizawa, a place in the mountains where many people went to escape the heat of the lowlands. It was October and the summer people had gone. I seemed to have the whole mountain to myself. God came to me so wonderfully with the promise in Zephaniah 3:17: "The Lord thy God in the midst of thee is mighty."

I had previously thought this verse meant that He was in the midst of the church. But He said, "No, I'm in the midst of *you;* I have come as your indwelling God, and My resurrection life is flowing through every nerve of your body, every organ. Just trust Me." I kept repeating His promise over and over-and believing it. He so perfectly healed me that I scarcely realized I had a nerve in my body!

I waited much on the Lord, but still the self-life bothered me.

Satan tormented me greatly in those days, saying, "Yes, you thought that if you stayed in Japan after the Board withdrew its support and trusted God and would be a glory to Him, everything would be all right. You will go home a nervous wreck and it will be the end of you." His Satanic screams were so loud that I would leave the house and walk up the mountain. From the top of the mountain I would cry out to the limit of my voice, "I will not doubt. All you devils in hell, listen! I will not doubt! My God will make Himself known to the Japanese people through me!"

One morning when I was walking on the mountain God spoke to me with such clarity that even now it seems I can see the spot where I was when He said, "I will dwell in you and walk in you." "I—the living God—I will dwell in you and walk in you. It is not going to be you anymore; it will be I" (Second Corinthians 6:16). How my heart rejoiced at these precious words!

When I arose the next morning I decided to fast and pray. During this time of waiting on the Lord, He gave me these wonderful words: "If we have been planted together in the likeness of his death, we shall be also in the likeness of his resurrection" (Romans 6:5).

In the depths of my soul I knew that *self* had gone to the cross. I had been planted in the likeness of His death and was living in His resurrection power. Jesus Himself in His resurrection glory stepped with new fullness onto the throne of my heart. How I rejoiced over this victory in Christ! I had the assurance of these words: "I in them, and thou in me, that they may be made perfect in one" (John 17:23).

After this experience I returned to my work. Everything was different! Indeed, everything has been different ever since. Galatians 2:20 became reality: "I am crucified with Christ; nevertheless I live; yet not I, *but Christ liveth in me.*"

It was a new revelation to me that as I actually entered into Christ's death, I also entered into His resurrection. Dr. A. B. Simpson wrote a hymn that we often sing:

Yes, I'm living in the glory
As He promised in His Word;
I am dwelling in the heavenlies,
Living in the glory of the Lord.

One Sunday morning as I stepped into the church, God gave me another illuminating revelation, this time from Romans 7:4: "Wherefore, my brethren, ye also are become dead to the law by the body of Christ; that ye should be married to another, even to him who is raised from the dead, that we should bring forth fruit unto God."

All through the service God was saying: "Through the offering of My body you are made dead to the *old self* that you might be joined to another." I saw that through this new relationship, I had come to inherit all. His death was mine, His burial was mine, His resurrection was mine, His ascension was mine. He transferred all of this to me. I was to live in heavenly places in Christ.

I had always thought that when I died or when Jesus returns I (as a part of His church) would become His bride. He revealed to me that I am *now* His bride. I am already joined to him. "I am the vine," said Jesus, "ye are the branches" (John 15:5). Nothing or no one can separate me from this precious union.

This is how an old hymn expresses it:

His forever, only His;
Who the Lord and me shall part?
Ah! with what rest of bliss,
Christ can fill the trusting heart!

Heaven and earth may fade and flee,
Firstborn light in gloom decline;
But while God and I shall be –
I am His, and He is mine!

As God continued to teach me, He made very real Matthew 6:22: "The light of the body is the eye: if therefore thine eye be single, thy whole body shall be full of light." I was very conscious that I did not have a single eye, an eye to see God's glory only. I wanted a little glory myself. The cry of my heart was that of Gerhardt when he wrote:

Jesus, Thy boundless love to me
No thought can reach, no tongue declare;
Oh, knit my thankful heart to Thee,
And reign without a rival there!

At the same time I was conscious that there was a rival, much as I hated it—even *self.*

God teaches us in Luke 11:36, "If thy whole body therefore be full of light, having no part dark, the whole shall be full of light, as when the bright shining of a candle

doth give thee light." When self went to the cross I knew
that no part was left dark. It seemed as if a glorious light
had been turned on in my inner soul!

Self-Reflection Questions:

1. In what areas of your life do you still sense the "self-
   life" resisting full surrender to Christ? How can
   you invite God to reveal and help you crucify those
   aspects of self so that you can fully experience His
   resurrection life?

2. Have you experienced moments when God's
   presence and promises felt distant due to self-
   reliance or doubt? How can you trust more deeply
   in God's promise to dwell within you and live
   through you, as He assures in His Word?

3. When seeking spiritual growth, are you asking
   God to reveal not only the death of self but also
   the fullness of His resurrection power? How can
   you live more fully in the reality that Christ's
   death, burial, and resurrection are now yours as His
   follower?

CHAPTER 11

WHAT MAY BE THE MOST DIFFICULT LESSON ENROUTE TO VICTORY?

To face the fact that even my good traits must go to the cross!

Beloved, here is something that is very hard for us to see on our path to spiritual victory:
EVEN OUR SEEMING GOOD TRAITS MUST GO TO THE CROSS!

Many people thought they were being kind when they would say, "Miss Francis is such a loving person"—and I believed it, too!

It is true that I did many pleasant things. But God said, "Yes, you are very loving, but the trouble is you love yourself."

I was astonished; what did He mean?

At that time three girls lived with me. They should have been strong Christians, but they were spoiled. The Lord said to me: "You are like a mother who is spoiling her child. She thinks she loves the child if she gives him everything he wants. It is not that she loves the child but that it pleases her to do this." This vivid portrayal pierced my inner being like an arrow. I pleaded earnestly, "Lord, what can I do?"

He said, "Consign it to the cross."

From that moment on there was a tremendous difference in my life. This trait seemed to be the center of my self-life. So I learned that my self-life was not always some ugly thing, some mean thing. With true insight into my human spirit, God knew that I had been brought up in a loving home and that it pleased me to do nice things. He had put His finger on the root of my weakness—*myself!*

So self, whether good or bad, had to be denied. I cast myself on the Lord, filled with deep conviction of my lack of oneness with Him. Again He proved Himself my strong deliverer. Since that day that attitude in my heart has been different toward everyone. I recognized immediately when dealing with people that this trait of pleasing self was gone. In times past when I had been talking to someone I liked and someone interrupted us, I had an inner uprising within me. Complete deliverance was now mine; interruptions were accepted as from the Lord.

As I entered into Christ's death, it was as the apostle Paul wrote: "I am crucified with Christ: nevertheless I live; yet not I, but Christ liveth in me: and the life which I now live in the flesh I live by the faith of the Son of God, who loved me, and gave himself for Me" (Galatians 2:20). He lived within. Oh, the blessedness of this relationship with the risen Christ in all His fullness!

His death had become my death; His burial had become mine; His resurrection had become mine; His ascension had become mine. I now live in heavenly places in Christ—the result of inwardly surrendering everything to Jesus.

Another experience that God used in leading me into this blessed mystery of the indwelling Christ came one day when a group of Japanese young people and I were singing that wonderful hymn by George Matheson:

Make me a captive, Lord,
And then I shall be free;
Force me to render up my sword,
And I shall conqueror be.

All at once God revealed to me that when anything struck against *myself* I would immediately take a vindicatory stand.

The words of the hymn so overwhelmed me that I had to go into another room and kneel before the Lord. I cried out to Him: "I have sung this song so many times before, but I never realized I had a sword; Lord, I surrender it to Thee." Gently He took it. Later, I realized I had no sword from that time onward.

Self-Reflection Questions:

1. What "good traits" in your life, such as kindness or generosity, might actually be rooted in self-pleasing rather than a desire to truly honor God? How can you surrender even these positive traits to the cross for His transformation?

2. Are there situations in your life where you feel the need to defend or vindicate yourself when challenged? How can you release the "sword" of self-defense and trust God to handle those moments for you?

3. How can you invite Christ to live more fully in and through you, as described in Galatians 2:20, so that even in your day-to-day interactions, His love and humility replace any remnants of self-focus?

CHAPTER 12

WHEN CAN I EXPECT FULL VICTORY OVER SELF?

When the resurrected Christ has taken over without a rival.

Many people who come forward in our services indicate that they are troubled by some outcropping of the old life of self.

I have sometimes asked them, "What do you do when these uprisings of self come?" Invariably their answer has been that they felt they had failed God. They had felt downcast and had wept and repented until peace came. I knew about this so well from my own experiences. But this is God showing us "self" for a purpose. This is cause for thankfulness. Self is not sin and will continue with us. We were born with this nature and we are not responsible for its failures. However, we are responsible if we let self, rather than the blessed Holy Spirit, take over and control us.

It seems natural to expect a wonderful, miraculous, and instantaneous deliverance. "Step by step you will be delivered," were God's words to me. Isaiah 1:25 became very real: "I will . . . thoroughly purge away your dross" (Amplified). In the final analysis, deliverance was instantaneously effective when

He entered all the doors I opened to Him to take over my entire life!

For so long I did not know that the life of victory I now live was possible. In fact, had someone told me I could not have understood the blessed reality of "forever one with Him." I believe the greatest day of my life, except for my salvation, was when I knew that the resurrected Christ had really taken over without a rival—that He was Lord of all in my whole being!

Oh, the rest of soul! All is His and He is mine forever and forever. No words can express the joy and peace of the heart in which Christ dwells as Lord.

John 15 teaches about the abiding life. As the branch we draw sustenance and strength from the vine—the Lord Jesus. Fruitfulness arises spontaneously from this abiding in the vine.

Have you experienced this reality? God will satisfy every desire that He puts in your heart. Your longings for Him will be fully satisfied. The words of Tersteegen's hymn offers praise to Him who is worthy:

> But I tell you I have seen Him,
> God's beloved Son,
> From His lips have learned the mystery
> He and His are one.
>
> There, as knit into the body
> Every joint and limb,
> We, His ransomed, His beloved,
> We are one with Him.

Hebrews 4:9-10 is a meaningful passage: "There remaineth therefore a *rest* to the people of God. For he that is entered into his rest, he also hath *ceased from his own works,* as God did from his." We can never enter into this marvelous rest as long as self has any place in our hearts. *Self* is an enemy within the camp. But oh, the joy when we can say from the heart:

Day by day His tender mercy
Healing, helping, full and free,
Sweet and strong, and oh, so patient,
Brought me lower while I whispered,
"Less of self and more of Thee."

Higher than the highest heavens,
Deeper than the deepest sea,
Lord, Thy love at last hath conquered:
Grant. me now my spirit's longing,
None of self and all of Thee.

Self-Reflection Questions:

1. In what areas of your life do you still experience "uprisings of self"? How do you typically respond, and how can you shift your perspective to see these moments as opportunities for God to reveal and purify self through His Spirit?

2. What doors in your heart are you keeping closed to Christ? How can you invite the resurrected Christ to take over every aspect of your life, allowing Him to be "Lord of all" without a rival?

3. How do you currently seek rest and peace in your spiritual life? What steps can you take to more fully abide in Christ, letting go of self-effort and allowing His strength and sustenance to flow through you?

www.ingramcontent.com/pod-product-compliance
Lightning Source LLC
Chambersburg PA
CBHW060349050426
42449CB00011B/2896